HAL•LEONARD
INSTRUMENTAL
PLAY-ALONG

AUDIO
ACCESS
INCLUDED

PLAYBACK+
Speed • Pitch • Balance • Loop

VIOLIN

SONGS FROM
A STAR IS BORN • LA
THE GREATEST SHOWMAN
AND MORE

MOVIE MUSICALS

Audio Arrangements by Peter Deneff

To access audio visit:
www.halleonard.com/mylibrary

Enter Code
7112-3884-6212-2111

ISBN 978-1-5400-4409-9

HAL•LEONARD®

Visit Hal Leonard Online at
www.halleonard.com

Contact us:
Hal Leonard
7777 West Bluemound Road
Milwaukee, WI 53213
Email: info@halleonard.com

In Europe, contact:
Hal Leonard Europe Limited
42 Wigmore Street
Marylebone, London, W1U 2RN
Email: info@halleonardeurope.com

In Australia, contact:
Hal Leonard Australia Pty. Ltd.
4 Lentara Court
Cheltenham, Victoria, 3192 Australia
Email: info@halleonard.com.au

THE GREATEST SHOWMAN

LA LA LAND

LES MISÉRABLES

MAMMA MIA! HERE WE GO AGAIN

A STAR IS BORN

THIS IS ME
from THE GREATEST SHOWMAN

VIOLIN

Words and Music by BENJ PASEK
and JUSTIN PAUL

A MILLION DREAMS
from THE GREATEST SHOWMAN

VIOLIN

Words and Music by BENJ PASEK
and JUSTIN PAUL

I DREAMED A DREAM
from LES MISÉRABLES

Violin

Music by CLAUDE-MICHEL SCHÖNBERG
Lyrics by ALAIN BOUBLIL, JEAN-MARC NATEL
and HERBERT KRETZMER

ANOTHER DAY OF SUN

from LA LA LAND

VIOLIN

Music by JUSTIN HURWITZ
Lyrics by BENJ PASEK & JUSTIN PAUL

CITY OF STARS

from LA LA LAND

VIOLIN

Music by JUSTIN HURWITZ
Lyrics by BENJ PASEK & JUSTIN PAUL

SOMEONE IN THE CROWD

from LA LA LAND

Violin

Music by JUSTIN HURWITZ
Lyrics by BENJ PASEK & JUSTIN PAUL

MAMMA MIA

featured in MAMMA MIA! HERE WE GO AGAIN

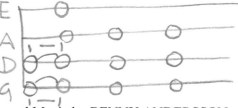

VIOLIN

Words and Music by BENNY ANDERSSON,
BJÖRN ULVAEUS and STIG ANDERSON

ALWAYS REMEMBER US THIS WAY

from *A STAR IS BORN*

VIOLIN

Words and Music by STEFANI GERMANOTTA,
HILLARY LINDSEY, NATALIE HEMBY
and LORI MCKENNA

I'LL NEVER LOVE AGAIN

from A STAR IS BORN

Violin

Words and Music by STEFANI GERMANOTTA,
AARON RAITIERE, HILLARY LINDSEY
and NATALIE HEMBY

LOOK WHAT I FOUND
from A STAR IS BORN

Violin

Words and Music by STEFANI GERMANOTTA,
AARON RAITIERE, NICK MONSON, LUKAS NELSON,
MARK NILAN, JR. and PAUL BLAIR

MAYBE IT'S TIME

from A STAR IS BORN

VIOLIN

Words and Music by
MICHAEL ISBELL

SHALLOW

from A STAR IS BORN

Violin

Words and Music by STEFANI GERMANOTTA,
MARK RONSON, ANDREW WYATT
and ANTHONY ROSSOMANDO

Your favorite songs are arranged just for solo instrumentalists with this outstanding series. Each book includes great full-accompaniment play-along audio so you can sound just like a pro! Check out **www.halleonard.com** to see all the titles available.

The Beatles

All You Need Is Love • Blackbird • Day Tripper • Eleanor Rigby • Get Back • Here, There and Everywhere • Hey Jude • I Will • Let It Be • Lucy in the Sky with Diamonds • Ob-La-Di, Ob-La-Da • Penny Lane • Something • Ticket to Ride • Yesterday.

_____00225330	Flute	$14.99
_____00225331	Clarinet	$14.99
_____00225332	Alto Sax	$14.99
_____00225333	Tenor Sax	$14.99
_____00225334	Trumpet	$14.99
_____00225335	Horn	$14.99
_____00225336	Trombone	$14.99
_____00225337	Violin	$14.99
_____00225338	Viola	$14.99
_____00225339	Cello	$14.99

Chart Hits

All About That Bass • All of Me • Happy • Radioactive • Roar • Say Something • Shake It Off • A Sky Full of Stars • Someone like You • Stay with Me • Thinking Out Loud • Uptown Funk.

_____00146207	Flute	$12.99
_____00146208	Clarinet	$12.99
_____00146209	Alto Sax	$12.99
_____00146210	Tenor Sax	$12.99
_____00146211	Trumpet	$12.99
_____00146212	Horn	$12.99
_____00146213	Trombone	$12.99
_____00146214	Violin	$12.99
_____00146215	Viola	$12.99
_____00146216	Cello	$12.99

Disney Greats

Arabian Nights • Hawaiian Roller Coaster Ride • It's a Small World • Look Through My Eyes • Yo Ho (A Pirate's Life for Me) • and more.

_____00841934	Flute	$12.99
_____00841935	Clarinet	$12.99
_____00841936	Alto Sax	$12.99
_____00841937	Tenor Sax	$12.95
_____00841938	Trumpet	$12.99
_____00841939	Horn	$12.99
_____00841940	Trombone	$12.99
_____00841941	Violin	$12.99
_____00841942	Viola	$12.99
_____00841943	Cello	$12.99
_____00842078	Oboe	$12.99

The Greatest Showman

Come Alive • From Now On • The Greatest Show • A Million Dreams • Never Enough • The Other Side • Rewrite the Stars • This Is Me • Tightrope.

_____00277389	Flute	$14.99
_____00277390	Clarinet	$14.99
_____00277391	Alto Sax	$14.99
_____00277392	Tenor Sax	$14.99
_____00277393	Trumpet	$14.99
_____00277394	Horn	$14.99
_____00277395	Trombone	$14.99
_____00277396	Violin	$14.99
_____00277397	Viola	$14.99
_____00277398	Cello	$14.99

Movie and TV Music

The Avengers • Doctor Who XI • Downton Abbey • Game of Thrones • Guardians of the Galaxy • Hawaii Five-O • Married Life • Rey's Theme (from *Star Wars: The Force Awakens*) • The X-Files • and more.

_____00261807	Flute	$12.99
_____00261808	Clarinet	$12.99
_____00261809	Alto Sax	$12.99
_____00261810	Tenor Sax	$12.99
_____00261811	Trumpet	$12.99
_____00261812	Horn	$12.99
_____00261813	Trombone	$12.99
_____00261814	Violin	$12.99
_____00261815	Viola	$12.99
_____00261816	Cello	$12.99

12 Pop Hits

Believer • Can't Stop the Feeling • Despacito • It Ain't Me • Look What You Made Me Do • Million Reasons • Perfect • Send My Love (To Your New Lover) • Shape of You • Slow Hands • Too Good at Goodbyes • What About Us.

_____00261790	Flute	$12.99
_____00261791	Clarinet	$12.99
_____00261792	Alto Sax	$12.99
_____00261793	Tenor Sax	$12.99
_____00261794	Trumpet	$12.99
_____00261795	Horn	$12.99
_____00261796	Trombone	$12.99
_____00261797	Violin	$12.99
_____00261798	Viola	$12.99
_____00261799	Cello	$12.99

Songs from Frozen, Tangled and Enchanted

Do You Want to Build a Snowman? • For the First Time in Forever • Happy Working Song • I See the Light • In Summer • Let It Go • Mother Knows Best • That's How You Know • True Love's First Kiss • When Will My Life Begin • and more.

_____00126921	Flute	$14.99
_____00126922	Clarinet	$14.99
_____00126923	Alto Sax	$14.99
_____00126924	Tenor Sax	$14.99
_____00126925	Trumpet	$14.99
_____00126926	Horn	$14.99
_____00126927	Trombone	$14.99
_____00126928	Violin	$14.99
_____00126929	Viola	$14.99
_____00126930	Cello	$14.99

Top Hits

Adventure of a Lifetime • Budapest • Die a Happy Man • Ex's & Oh's • Fight Song • Hello • Let It Go • Love Yourself • One Call Away • Pillowtalk • Stitches • Writing's on the Wall.

_____00171073	Flute	$12.99
_____00171074	Clarinet	$12.99
_____00171075	Alto Sax	$12.99
_____00171106	Tenor Sax	$12.99
_____00171107	Trumpet	$12.99
_____00171108	Horn	$12.99
_____00171109	Trombone	$12.99
_____00171110	Violin	$12.99
_____00171111	Viola	$12.99
_____00171112	Cello	$12.99

Wicked

As Long As You're Mine • Dancing Through Life • Defying Gravity • For Good • I'm Not That Girl • Popular • The Wizard and I • and more.

_____00842236	Flute	$12.99
_____00842237	Clarinet	$12.99
_____00842238	Alto Saxophone	$12.99
_____00842239	Tenor Saxophone	$11.95
_____00842240	Trumpet	$12.99
_____00842241	Horn	$12.99
_____00842242	Trombone	$12.99
_____00842243	Violin	$12.99
_____00842244	Viola	$12.99
_____00842245	Cello	$12.99

HAL•LEONARD®

101 SONGS

BIG COLLECTIONS OF FAVORITE SONGS ARRANGED FOR SOLO INSTRUMENTALISTS.

101 BROADWAY SONGS

00154199	Flute	$14.99
00154200	Clarinet	$14.99
00154201	Alto Sax	$14.99
00154202	Tenor Sax	$14.99
00154203	Trumpet	$14.99
00154204	Horn	$14.99
00154205	Trombone	$14.99
00154206	Violin	$14.99
00154207	Viola	$14.99
00154208	Cello	$14.99

101 HIT SONGS

00194561	Flute	$16.99
00197182	Clarinet	$16.99
00197183	Alto Sax	$16.99
00197184	Tenor Sax	$16.99
00197185	Trumpet	$16.99
00197186	Horn	$16.99
00197187	Trombone	$16.99
00197188	Violin	$16.99
00197189	Viola	$16.99
00197190	Cello	$16.99

101 CHRISTMAS SONGS

00278637	Flute	$14.99
00278638	Clarinet	$14.99
00278639	Alto Sax	$14.99
00278640	Tenor Sax	$14.99
00278641	Trumpet	$14.99
00278642	Horn	$14.99
00278643	Trombone	$14.99
00278644	Violin	$14.99
00278645	Viola	$14.99
00278646	Cello	$14.99

101 JAZZ SONGS

00146363	Flute	$14.99
00146364	Clarinet	$14.99
00146366	Alto Sax	$14.99
00146367	Tenor Sax	$14.99
00146368	Trumpet	$14.99
00146369	Horn	$14.99
00146370	Trombone	$14.99
00146371	Violin	$14.99
00146372	Viola	$14.99
00146373	Cello	$14.99

101 CLASSICAL THEMES

00155315	Flute	$14.99
00155317	Clarinet	$14.99
00155318	Alto Sax	$14.99
00155319	Tenor Sax	$14.99
00155320	Trumpet	$14.99
00155321	Horn	$14.99
00155322	Trombone	$14.99
00155323	Violin	$14.99
00155324	Viola	$14.99
00155325	Cello	$14.99

101 MOVIE HITS

00158087	Flute	$14.99
00158088	Clarinet	$14.99
00158089	Alto Sax	$14.99
00158090	Tenor Sax	$14.99
00158091	Trumpet	$14.99
00158092	Horn	$14.99
00158093	Trombone	$14.99
00158094	Violin	$14.99
00158095	Viola	$14.99
00158096	Cello	$14.99

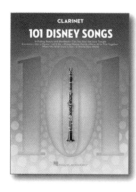

101 DISNEY SONGS

00244104	Flute	$16.99
00244106	Clarinet	$16.99
00244107	Alto Sax	$16.99
00244108	Tenor Sax	$16.99
00244109	Trumpet	$16.99
00244112	Horn	$16.99
00244120	Trombone	$16.99
00244121	Violin	$16.99
00244125	Viola	$16.99
00244126	Cello	$16.99

101 POPULAR SONGS

00224722	Flute	$16.99
00224723	Clarinet	$16.99
00224724	Alto Sax	$16.99
00224725	Tenor Sax	$16.99
00224726	Trumpet	$16.99
00224727	Horn	$16.99
00224728	Trombone	$16.99
00224729	Violin	$16.99
00224730	Viola	$16.99
00224731	Cello	$16.99

HAL•LEONARD®
www.halleonard.com